Consolidated B–24J Liberator, 308th Bomb Group, 375th Bomb Squadron, 14th Air Force, CBI. Black under surfaces, red mouth outlined dark blue.

Consolidated B–24J Liberator, 90th Bomb Group, 5th Air Force, South West Pacific Area. Natural metal finish, red mouth outlined dark blue. OD fin with white 'Skull and Crossbombs', blue vertical stripe, red white horizontal stripes on rudder.

SHARKMOUTH 1945-1970

Illustrated and Compiled by Richard Ward

ACKNOWLEDGEMENTS

I should like to thank the many friends who have over the past five years or so assisted me with the collecting of photographs and information relating to the SHARK-MOUTH and to variations of this marking. My thanks to all who helped; their names are listed below in alphabetical order. Probably a word about the layout of the books may not be out of place here. The layout finally chosen after much thought is partly chronological and partly by type and/or unit, the lapses being dictated by the space available and the large amount of material which had to be included. I make no apology for the duplication of certain photographs and illustrations which have appeared in earlier AIRCAM publications, for obvious reasons.

Ches Agee, Peter M. Bowers, R. A. Brown, R. M. Bueschel, K. Buchanan, Jack Canary, M. R. vaz Carneiro, G. Cattaneo, J. Cuny, J. Geer, Dr. J. G. Handelman, L. B. Hansen, R. W. Harrison, E. Hart, Borge Heilm, R. M. Hill, H. Hooftman, Gerhard Joos, D. A. Kasulka, Andras Kelemen, N. Krane, G. J. Letzter, W. Liss, D. W. Menard, E. R. McDowell, E. Munday, H. J. Nowarra, S. P. Peltz, Earl Reinert, K. Shabo, Frank F. Smith, Stan Staples, Jose Villela Jr., Bell Helicopter Co., Grumman Aerospace Corp., North American Aviation, Imperial War Museum, Etablissement Cinematographique des Armées, Royal Air Force, United States Air Force, United States Marine Corps, United States Navy.

Vought F8U–1 Crusader, VF–32, US Navy. Red mouth and lips, yellow tail stripes outlined with black, otherwise standard colour scheme and markings.

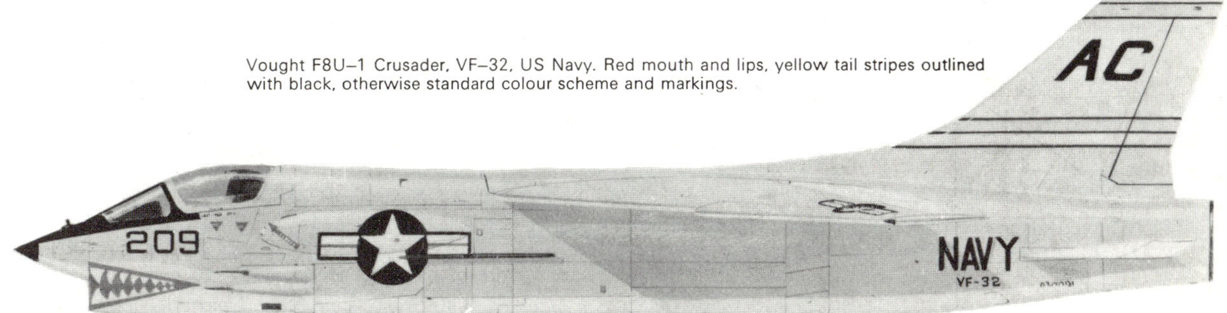

Published by: Osprey Publications Limited, England
Editorial Office: P.O. Box 5, Canterbury, Kent, England
Subscription & Business Office: P.O. Box 25, 707 Oxford Road, Reading, Berkshire, England

The Berkshire Printing Co., Ltd.   ©   Osprey Publications Ltd. SBN 85045 015 2

'Frank' a 15th Air Force bomb group mascot warily inspects the massive Sharkmouth on the nose of 'Howling Wolf'. Unit unknown, Italy 1944.   (USAF)

Close-up detail of the Sharkmouth on the nose of the 458th Bomb Group formating ship. Certainly more Liberators than any other multi-engined type carried the marking during World War II. Note whip aerials. (USAF)

SHARKMOUTH 1945-1970

During the post-war years many unit and individual sharkmouth designs have come and gone. Until their final disbandment as an operational fighter squadron, No. 112 Squadron, R.A.F., were the most consistent users of the insignia; and there is a rumour that even after disbandment the sharkmouth refused to die, re-appearing on a new type of background when the unit was re-formed for the fourth time as a Home Defence Bloodhound missile squadron!

The 51st Fighter Group retained their sharkmouth until disbanded in December 1945. It is not known if the insignia was resurrected on the P-47 and P-61 aircraft with which the unit was equipped when it was re-activated in October 1946; the next confirmed use of the sharkmouth on 51st Fighter Interceptor aircraft occured towards the end of the Korean War, when the group was equipped with North American F-86F Sabres; the design was retained subsequently in Japan and Okinawa.

The Philippine, Dominican and Colombian Air Forces have certainly operated F-51 Mustangs in unit strength with the sharkmouth much in evidence; indeed, at the beginning of 1970 the Colombians still have one squadron of sharkmouthed Mustangs operational. Unexpectedly the Mexican Air Force approved the use of the marking on their newly-acquired D.H. Vampire FB.4's, equipping No. 200 Fighter Squadron; this is the first known use of the sharkmouth by the Mexicans. During the mid‑1950's the insignia appeared on the Dassault Ouragans of the Israeli Defence Force/Air Force, one of the most vigorous and formidable of the world's younger air arms. The West German *Luftwaffe* unit, LEKG 41, used the design as a unit marking for a brief period; their Fiat G.91R's carried the sharkmouth during the NATO Bulls Eye Competition in the summer of 1969.

Over the past few years honours appear to be roughly even between the U.S.A.F. and the U.S. Navy, as to the number of units flying sharkmouth aircraft; if anything, the balance is slightly in favour of the U.S. Navy, a reversal of the position existing during the war years. In 1969 the mouth appeared on Bell AH-1G Huey Cobra helicopter gun‑ships, and no doubt this will not be the last time some variation of this historic and evocative aircraft marking is flown into combat by one of the world's air forces or naval air arms. One thing is certain; the pilots who fly the sharkmouths in future campaigns will be hard put to it to surpass the record of the men who wrote earlier chapters of the sharkmouth story — for the tradition is built on a foundation of gravestones and medals, second to none.

Above: B–24J of the 448th Bomb Group, 8th Air Force, ETO, commanded by Colonel Charles B. Westover, takes off from its base in England with a bomb-bay loaded with supplies to be dropped by parachute to airborne troops fighting east of the Rhine. (USAF)

Right: This B–24J of the 93rd Bomb Group, 330th Bomb Squadron, 8th Air Force, flown by Lt. Ches Agee ran out of runway through lack of brakes due to flak damage over Germany. The mouth in actual fact was supposed to represent a Whalemouth and not a shark. Code AG＋L, serial unknown. (Ches Agee via Stan Staples)

Above: Formating Liberator of the 458th Bomb Group. See colour illustration. (USAF via E. Munday)

Above & below: A pair of B–24J's of the 458th Bomb Group await take-off for the 200th mission, 26th February 1945. See colour illustration. (Photos USAF)

Above left: Sharkmouthed Liberators of the 489th Bomb Group, photo taken during an attack on Frankfurt, 4.2.44, note stick of bombs falling between the two Libs and photo aircraft. (IWM)

Above right: B–24L probably of the 308th Bomb Group, 14th Air Force, CBI, on an Indian airfield, 1945. See colour illustration. (Peter M. Bowers)

Above: Close-up of typical 90th. Bomb Group 'Skull & Cross Bombs' insignia. (via E. R. McDowell)

Left: B–24J's of the 90th Bomb Group, 5th Air Force, SWPA. Aircraft with Sharkmouth is believed to be 407, see colour illustration. (Frank F. Smith)

Below: Nice shot of an OD and grey B–24J of the 90th Bomb Group coming into land on an airfield on Biak, 1944. (Norb Krane via R. M. Hill)

Bottom: Natural metal B–24J of the 90th Bomb Group, full colour details of this aircraft will be found in AIRCAM No. 11 Vol. 1. Fin is OD with 90th BG insignia in white, rudder with blue vertical stripe and red and white horizontal stripes, a/c number 785 in white above skull. (via Frank F. Smith)

Above: B–24J's of the 308th BG, 375th BS, 14th AF, leaving Hankow airfield in ruins on the 18th December 1944, date of the first combined 14th and 20th AF raids, B–29's of the 20th AF raided the Hankow industrial centre and waterfront at the same time. Nearest aircraft complete with Sharkmouth, serial 440832 on fin with 483 below, both in black. (USAF)

Above: B–24J of the 375th Bomb Squadron landing at Kweilin, south-central China, see AIRCAM No. 11 Vol. 1 for colour details. (Jack Canary via R. M. Bueschel)

Above & below: Selection of Sharkmouths and other nose decor on Liberators of the 308th Bomb Group, 14th Air Force, CBI. (Eric Hart via R. M. Hill)

Below: 'Bitch's Sister' an OD and grey B–24J of the 308th Bomb Group in its dispersal area at Kweilin airfield, China. Serial in yellow on fin 273319 with 505 below. (Eric Hart via R. M. Hill)

Above: A B–24J Liberator leaving Hengyang after bombing supply dump on outskirts of city on 16th September 1944. 375th Bomb Squadron, serial 440584. (USAF)

Below: 'Esky' of the 308th BS with collapsed port undercart after running out of runway at Kweilin. (via E. R. McDowell)

Below: Line-up of 375th BG Liberators on Nanning airfield, China. In this instance their role was that of transports, not bombers, having flown in with a load of gas to keep the fighters operational. 16th November 1944. (USAF)

Below: 'Barracuda' a Sharkmouthed B–26B Marauder of the 344th Bomb Group, 9th Air Force, ETO. Photo taken on Beauvais-Tille airfield, France, March 1945. Natural metal scheme with white triangle on fin and rudder, serial 2107585, code unknown. (via R. W. Harrison)

Above: Martin B–26B Marauder of the 397th Bomb Group, 599th Bomb Squadron, 9th Air Force, ETO. See colour illustration. (IWM)

Below: Sharkmouth B–26 Marauder of an unknown unit of the 12th Air Force, MTO. OD and grey scheme, red mouth, white teeth and black lips, white 95 on fin, serial 243304 in yellow. There is another photograph of this aircraft in the files of the IWM taken during the same raid but from ahead and above, neg. number EA24353. (IWM)

Below: Another 12th Air Force Marauder of an unknown unit in Italy.

Fine selection of photographs of a B–25H Mitchell of the AAF Tactical Center, Orlando Field, Florida. Red mouth, white teeth, red lips and blood drips; aircraft is painted in the early USAAF maritime scheme, see colour illustration. (Photo USAF)

Above: Sharkmouthed B–25C Mitchell, the 10th aircraft modified with solid nose. 'Mortimer' on nose in white, row of five Jap flags under cockpit, serial 112443. Unit unknown.

Above & below left: Trio of F–10 Mitchells from an unknown unit based in the Caribbean area, photos taken over Cuba. See colour illustration. (USAF)

Below, two pictures: Port side close-ups of 'Bones' looking like some prehistoric reptile. (via André ver Elst)

Below: 'Bones' the last B–25 to come off the production line at North American's Inglewood plant, covered from nose to tail with the signatures of employees. Mouth and spinners red, teeth white, lips black, very crudely painted on, 'Bones' in black, serial 35104. 12th Bomb Group, 81st Bomb Squadron, 10th Air Force, CBI. (USAF)

Above: A B–25J Mitchell of the 'Air Apaches' attacking Japanese troop concentrations and supply dumps in Humbolt Bay, New Guinea. 345th Bomb Group 'Air Apaches', 499th Bomb Squadron 'Bats Outa Hell', 5th Air Force. (USAF)

Below: Sharkmouthed B–25 Mitchell attacking a convoy off Keviang, New Ireland. Note Mitchell between the masts of the cargo boat which was sunk. From the wake of the Jap escort vessel apparently evasive action did not figure in the captain's book of tactics. Unit unknown. (USAF)

Above: B–25H Mitchell of the 12th Bomb Group on an Indian airfield, see colour illustration. (Peter M. Bowers)

Above: Another Mitchell of the 12th Bomb Group landing on an Indian airfield, note lake in foreground due to monsoon rains. (USAF)

Above & below: Mouths and other nose decor of various Mitchells of the 12th Bomb Group, 10th Air Force, CBI. (via E. R. McDowell)

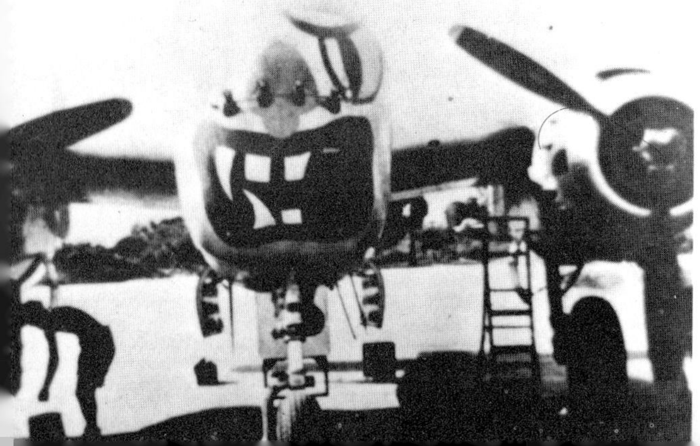

Above: B–24J Mitchell, 345th Bomb Group 'Air Apaches', 499th Bomb Squadron 'Bats Outa Hell', 5th Air Force. See colour illustration. (via E. R. McDowell)

Right: Close-up showing the Batmouth and armament in detail. (via E. R. McDowell)

Below: Only known Royal Australian Air Force Mitchell with a Sharkmouth, a Mk. III of No. 2 Squadron at Hughes Field, Northern Territory, June 1944. No. 2 Squadron code was KO but neither code nor serial is known. (via Frank F. Smith)

Right: 'Butcha' a Sharkmouthed A–20G Havoc of the 410th Bomb Group, 9th Air Force, ETO. The only known example of a 9th AF Havoc with the Sharkmouth, neither the code nor serial is known. Note D-Day Invasion stripes. (via Frank F. Smith)

Above: Ground-crew installing rocket tubes on a A–20G Havoc of the 417th Bomb Group, 5th Air Force, SWPA. Saidor, New Guinea. Red mouth and lips, white teeth and tip of fin and rudder. (USAF)

Above: Mouths and other nose decor of a pair of A–20G Havocs of the 417th BG, left 'Amourous Amazon' and right 'Scremen Demen'. (Photos Norb Krane via R. M. Hill)

Right & below: P–40N modified as a two-seater at Kangwan Field, 1946. OD and grey scheme, red/blue mouth, white teeth, thin blue lips, rudder blue and white stripes. A colour illustration of this Warhawk will be found in AIR-CAM No. 7. (Earl Reinert)

Above: Close-up of the Sharkmouth of a Yak 9D of the Normandie-Niemen Regiment, East Prussia/Northern Poland, 1944. (Witold Liss)

Right: Nose detail showing Sharkmouth of a Yak 9M also of the Normandie-Niemen Regiment, note French roundel under cockpit. The Normandie-Niemen Fighter Regiment was composed of Free French aircrew and Russian groundcrew and fought on the Eastern Front from 1943 to the end of hostilities in Europe, finishing the war with 273 confirmed kills. (Witold Liss)

Another Russian aircraft known to have had a Sharkmouth design on the cowl was a Lavochkin La 5; the quality of the only known photograph is too poor to reproduce here.

Below: A Handley-Page Halifax Series II with Sharkmouth and 'Saint', nothing is known of this aircraft. (via R. C. Jones)

Above: GA–Q FB241, a North American Mustang Mk. III of No. 112 'Shark' Squadron on an Italian airfield. Standard green/grey upper surfaces with pale grey under surfaces, Black/red mouth, white teeth, black lips.

Above: Line-up of Mk. III's of No. 112 'Shark' Squadron at Zarro, Yugoslavia, 1945. See AIRCAM No. 3 for colour details of GA–R.

Above both pictures: Mouth detail of a pair of 'A' Flight Mk. IV's of No. 112 Squadron. Note 500lb bombs on aircraft to right, shortly after this photo was taken the a/c aborted on a ground-attack op., returning to the airfield without jettisoning its bomb load, both bombs falling off and exploding on touch-down destroying the aircraft but damaging the pilot not at all.

Below: Very nice flying shot of KH774 a Mk. IV of No. 112 'Shark' Squadron, No. 239 Fighter Bomber Wing, Desert Air Force, based at Cervia, Italy, May 1945. See AIRCAM No. 3 for colour details of this aircraft.

Above: Only known 8th Air Force P–51B Mustang with a Sharkmouth, 352nd Fighter. Group, 487th Fighter Squadron, see colour illustration. (via K. Shabo)

Right: 'Big Mac Junior', a P–51B Mustang of the 363rd Fighter Group, 382nd Fighter Squadron, 9th Air Force, flown by Major J. R. Brown Jr. For colour details see AIRCAM No. 5

Above & below: 'Jeanne III' a colourful P–51B Mustang almost certainly of the 51st Fighter Group on the airfield at Kweilin in south-central China. Legend on the signpost reads 'Los Angeles City Limits'. See colour illustration. (Jack Canary via R. M. Bueschel)

Above: A P–51C of the 51st Fighter Group armed with rocket tubes waits on its dispersal area on a Chinese airfield for the next ground-attack mission against advancing Japanese forces. (Jack Canary via R. M. Bueschel)

Above: Line-up of Mustangs on a Chinese airfield, nearest P–51C with Sharkmouth 'Little Miss D' has three diagonal stripes round fuselage in the style of the 1st Air Commando Group and it may belong to this unit though it is doubtful. The other Mustangs with the black flash along the fuselage belong to the 118th TRS. (Jack Canary via R. M. Bueschel)

Above: P–51C of the 51st Fighter Group, 16th Fighter Squadron, 14th Air Force, CBI, on a Chinese airfield in July 1944. Note Bazooka tubes. (USAF)

Below: A P–51C probably of the 23rd FG on a Chinese airfield. Mouths in all cases are blue/red with white teeth and blue lips. (USAF)

Top: F–51D Mustang of the 18th Fighter Bomber Wing, 12th Fighter Bomber Squadron, FEAF, on the dispersal area at Pusan, Korea, September 1950. Note red wing, fin and rudder tip, red mouth, white teeth, black lips. (USAF)

Above: Another pair of F–51D's of the 12th Fighter Bomber Squadron on Pusan airfield during the Korean War. September 1950. (USAF)

Below: F–51D's of the 12th FBS and No. 2 'Flying Cheetah' Squadron, South African Air Force line up for assembly line armament reloads of HVR's and bombs. Pusan airfield, Korea, November 1951. (USAF)

Below: Refuelled and re-armed Mustangs of the 12th FBS and No. 2 SAAF taxying out for take-off on a Korean airfield in 1951. (USAF)

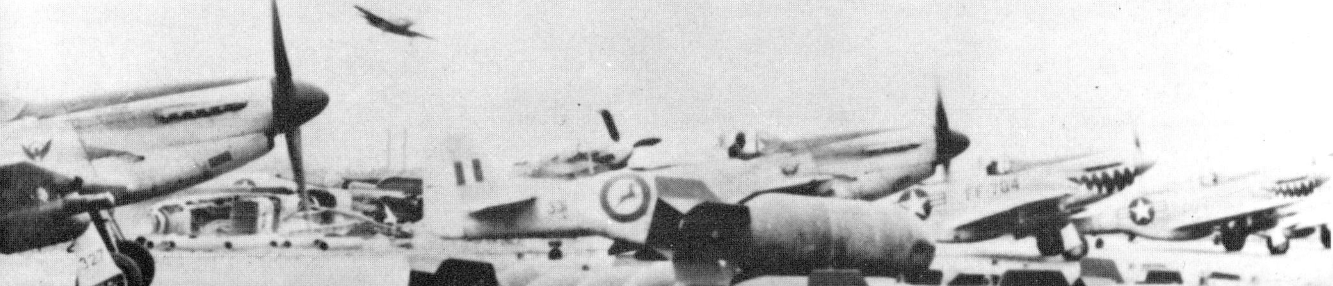

Above: F–51D of the West Virginia Air National Guard, see colour illustration. (R. W. Harrison)

Above: F–51H Mustang of the New Hampshire Air National Guard. (Brian Baker)

Above: Neat formation by Mustangs of the NEIAF, H3–315 nearest aircraft to camera with Sharkmouth, note eye aft and above exhaust ports. (via Hugo Hooftman)

Left & below left: F–51D Mustang one of two flown by Brigadier General B. N. Ebuen of the Philippine Air Force. See colour illustrations of both aircraft. (D. W. Menard)

Below: Insignia detail of 001. (D. W. Menard)

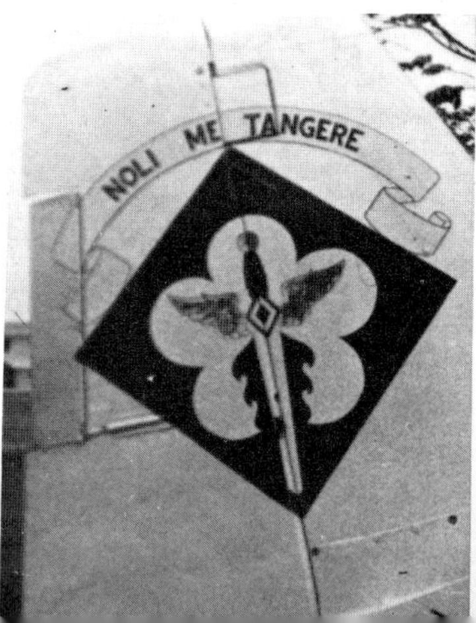

Above: Grumman F6F–3 Hellcat making a fitting background to this photograph of the aircrew of VF–27 at Maui, Hawaii, May 1944, prior to embarking aboard the USS Princeton CVL–23. (US Navy)

Right & below: Carl A. Brown landing his damaged F6F–5 Hellcat of VF–27 aboard the USS Essex CV–9 on 24th October 1944. The USS Princeton, VF–27's own ship, can be seen burning in the background. Brown had shot down five Japanese aircraft during this mission. (US Navy)

Above: Vought F4U–4 Corsair coming in to land aboard the USS Boxer CV–21 after strike against ground targets in Korea, 14th July 1952. 1st Marine Air Wing. Note 11 on landing gear covers, see colour illustration. (USMC)

Above: 'Flak Bait' a midnight blue Vought F4U–1 Corsair of an unknown Marine Corps unit on Ie Shima, June 1945. Main role of this particular Corsair at the time the photograph was taken was the defence of bases in the Okinawas against Kamikaze attacks. Drop tank is blue upper, grey under, red mouth, white teeth, blue lips. (USMC) ·

Below: Grumman F9F–3 Panther of VMF–311, 1st Marine Air Wing, being overhauled on airstrip K–3, Korea, 25th June 1951. See colour illustration. (USMC)

Above & below: North American T–6G Texan, 8th Escadre, EALA 13/72, Paul Cazelle Base, Essaouira, Central Algeria, 1957. The aircraft illustrated in colour was flown by the C.O., Cme. Verlet, and carried no code letters. An example with code letters is 93098 with WG in large square black letters, aft of and slightly smaller than the roundel, otherwise the colour scheme and markings were identical. (J. M. Cuny)

Right: Nose detail of Bf 109G–6 of Hlelv 31, Night-Fighter Flight, flown by Capt. Borge Heilm, Utti, 1948. Finnish Air Force. See colour illustration. (Capt. Borge Heilm)

Below: Very interesting Pilatus D.3801 (M.S.406) of the Swiss Air Force. Note 277 in white on leading edge of wings slightly inboard of main undercarriage leg. (Credit unknown)

Above: De Havilland Vampire FB.4 of Escuadron Aereo de Pelea 200, Mexican Air Force. See colour illustration. (Jose Villela Jr.)

Left: Close-up showing detail of unit insignia, in cockpit is Cor. P. A. Graco Ramirez Garrido, squadron C.O. (Jose Villela Jr.)

Below: Gloster Meteor F.4 of the Brazilian Air Force, see colour illustration. (Andras Kelemen via Mario Roberto vaz Carneiro)

Below: Cessna 01–E Bird Dog of the 19th Tactical Air Support Squadron, Bien Hoa Air Base, South Vietnam. Photograph taken in December 1945. Note very long whip aerial above cockpit. (D. W. Menard)

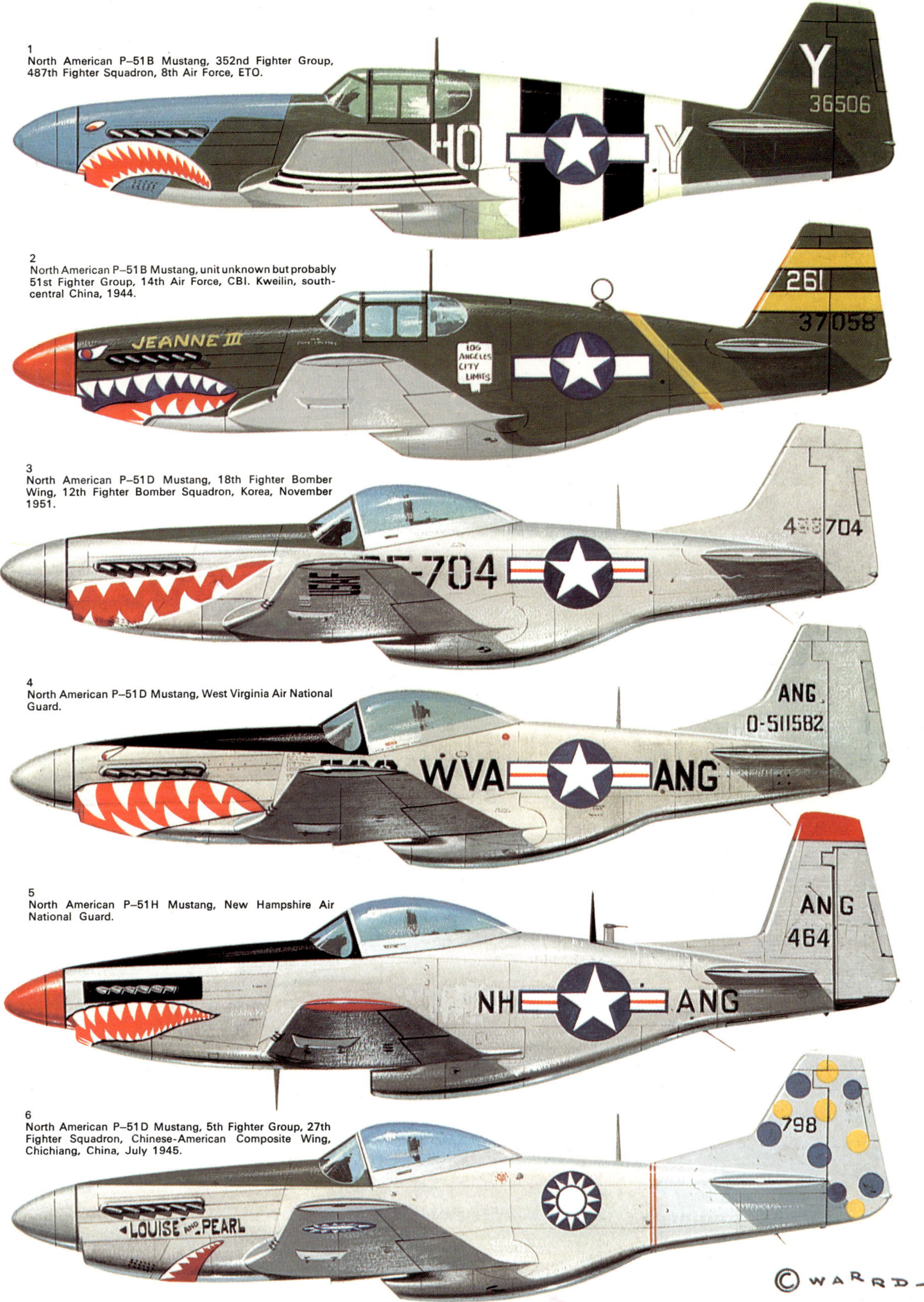

A

1
North American P–51B Mustang, 352nd Fighter Group,
487th Fighter Squadron, 8th Air Force, ETO.

2
North American P–51B Mustang, unit unknown but probably
51st Fighter Group, 14th Air Force, CBI. Kweilin, south-
central China, 1944.

3
North American P–51D Mustang, 18th Fighter Bomber
Wing, 12th Fighter Bomber Squadron, Korea, November
1951.

4
North American P–51D Mustang, West Virginia Air National
Guard.

5
North American P–51H Mustang, New Hampshire Air
National Guard.

6
North American P–51D Mustang, 5th Fighter Group, 27th
Fighter Squadron, Chinese-American Composite Wing,
Chichiang, China, July 1945.

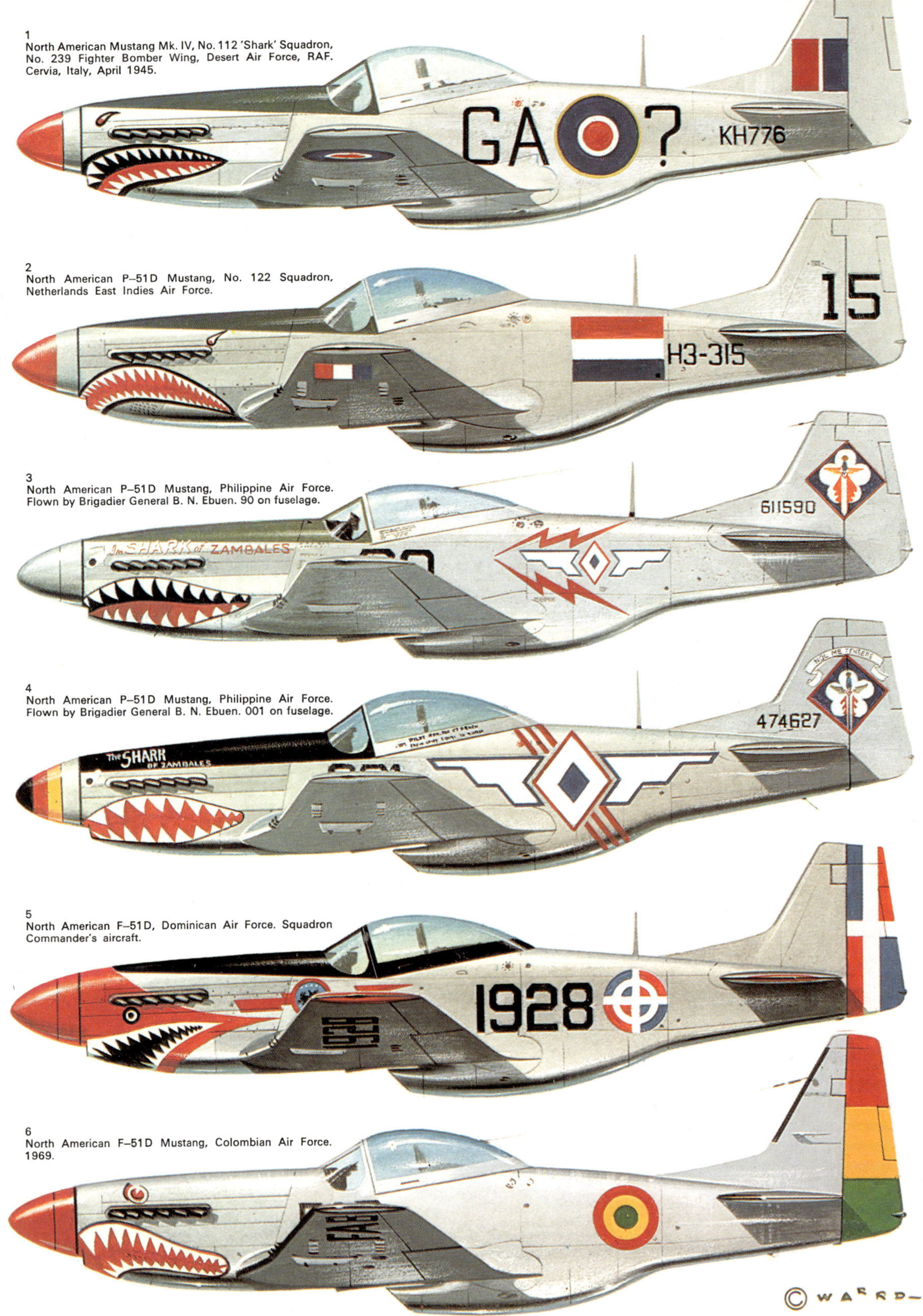

1
North American Mustang Mk. IV, No. 112 'Shark' Squadron, No. 239 Fighter Bomber Wing, Desert Air Force, RAF. Cervia, Italy, April 1945.

2
North American P–51D Mustang, No. 122 Squadron, Netherlands East Indies Air Force.

3
North American P–51D Mustang, Philippine Air Force. Flown by Brigadier General B. N. Ebuen. 90 on fuselage.

4
North American P–51D Mustang, Philippine Air Force. Flown by Brigadier General B. N. Ebuen. 001 on fuselage.

5
North American F–51D, Dominican Air Force. Squadron Commander's aircraft.

6
North American F–51D Mustang, Colombian Air Force. 1969.

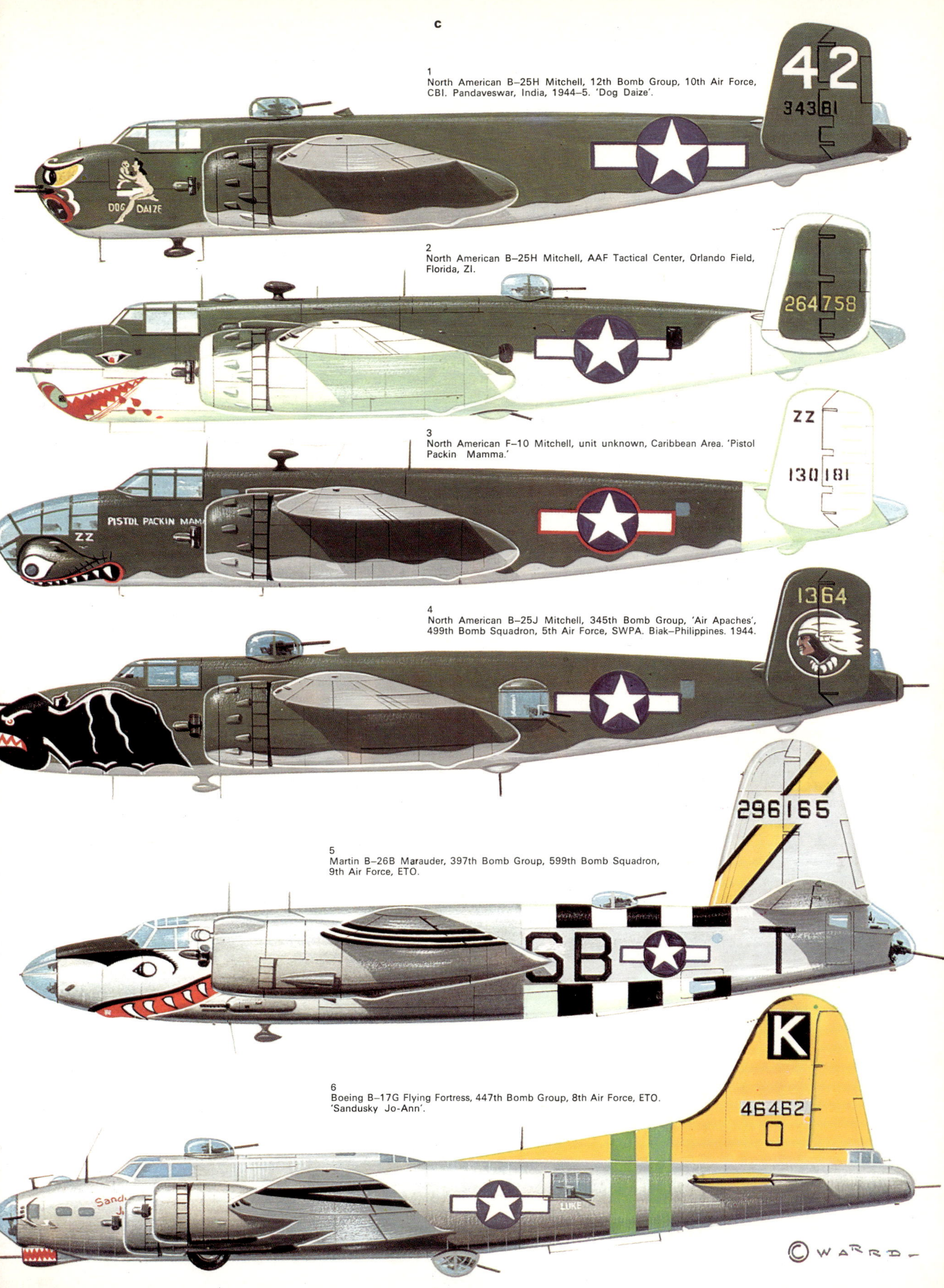

c

1
North American B–25H Mitchell, 12th Bomb Group, 10th Air Force, CBI. Pandaveswar, India, 1944–5. 'Dog Daize'.

2
North American B–25H Mitchell, AAF Tactical Center, Orlando Field, Florida, ZI.

3
North American F–10 Mitchell, unit unknown, Caribbean Area. 'Pistol Packin Mamma.'

4
North American B–25J Mitchell, 345th Bomb Group, 'Air Apaches', 499th Bomb Squadron, 5th Air Force, SWPA. Biak–Philippines. 1944.

5
Martin B–26B Marauder, 397th Bomb Group, 599th Bomb Squadron, 9th Air Force, ETO.

6
Boeing B–17G Flying Fortress, 447th Bomb Group, 8th Air Force, ETO. 'Sandusky Jo-Ann'.

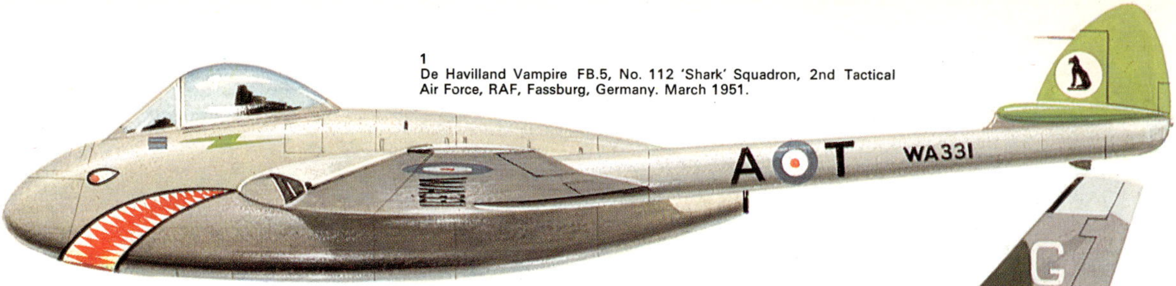

1
De Havilland Vampire FB.5, No. 112 'Shark' Squadron, 2nd Tactical
Air Force, RAF, Fassburg, Germany. March 1951.

2
Canadair Sabre F.4, No. 112 'Shark' Squadron, 2nd Tactical Air Force,
RAF, Bruggen, Germany, Jan.–Nov. 1955.

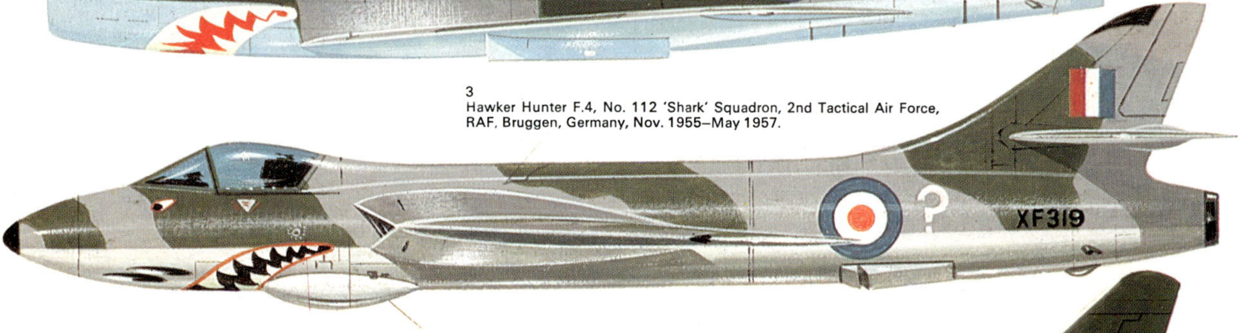

3
Hawker Hunter F.4, No. 112 'Shark' Squadron, 2nd Tactical Air Force,
RAF, Bruggen, Germany, Nov. 1955–May 1957.

4
Fiat G.91R/3, unit unknown, Luftwaffe.

5
Fiat G.91R/3, LEKG 41, Luftwaffe.

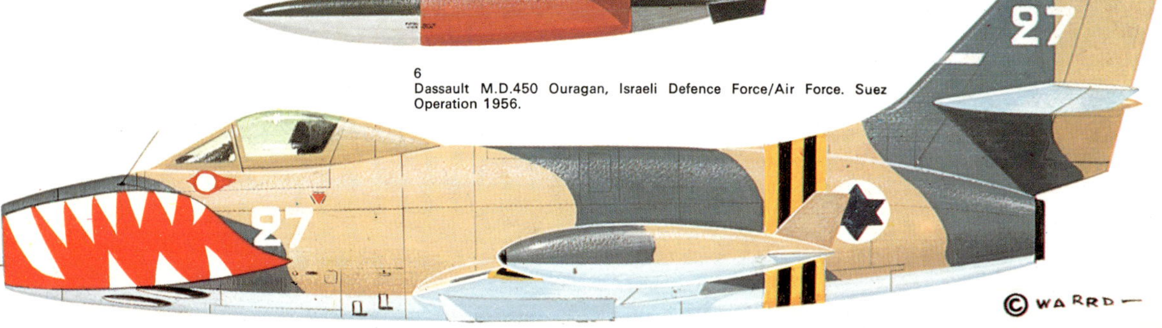

6
Dassault M.D.450 Ouragan, Israeli Defence Force/Air Force. Suez
Operation 1956.

1 De Havilland Vampire FB.4, No. 200 Fighter Squadron, Mexican Air Force, Squadron Commander's aircraft.

2 Gloster Meteor F—4, Argentine Air Force.

3 North American F—86F Sabre, Chinese Nationalist Air Force.

4 North American F—86F Sabre, 51st Fighter Interceptor Wing, Far East Air Force. Tsuiki Air Base, Japan. 1954.

5 North American F—86D Sabre, 408th Fighter Interceptor Wing, 520th Fighter Interceptor Squadron, Air Defence Command. Klamath MA, Oregon, 1956.

6 North American F—86K Sabre, No. 337 Squadron, Royal Norwegian Air Force.

1
Lockheed F–80A Shooting Star, unit unknown.

2
Lockheed F–94B, unit unknown. Sampson AFB, New York, 1953–4.

3
North American F–100D, 3rd Tactical Fighter Wing, 308th Tactical Fighter Squadron, Bien Hoa AB, South Vietnam. December 1965.

4
North American F–100C Super Sabre, 127th Tactical Fighter Squadron, Kansas Air National Guard. McConnell AFB, Kansas, 1969.

5
Republic F–105D Thunderchief, 23rd Tactical Fighter Wing, McConnell AFB, Kansas, 1964.

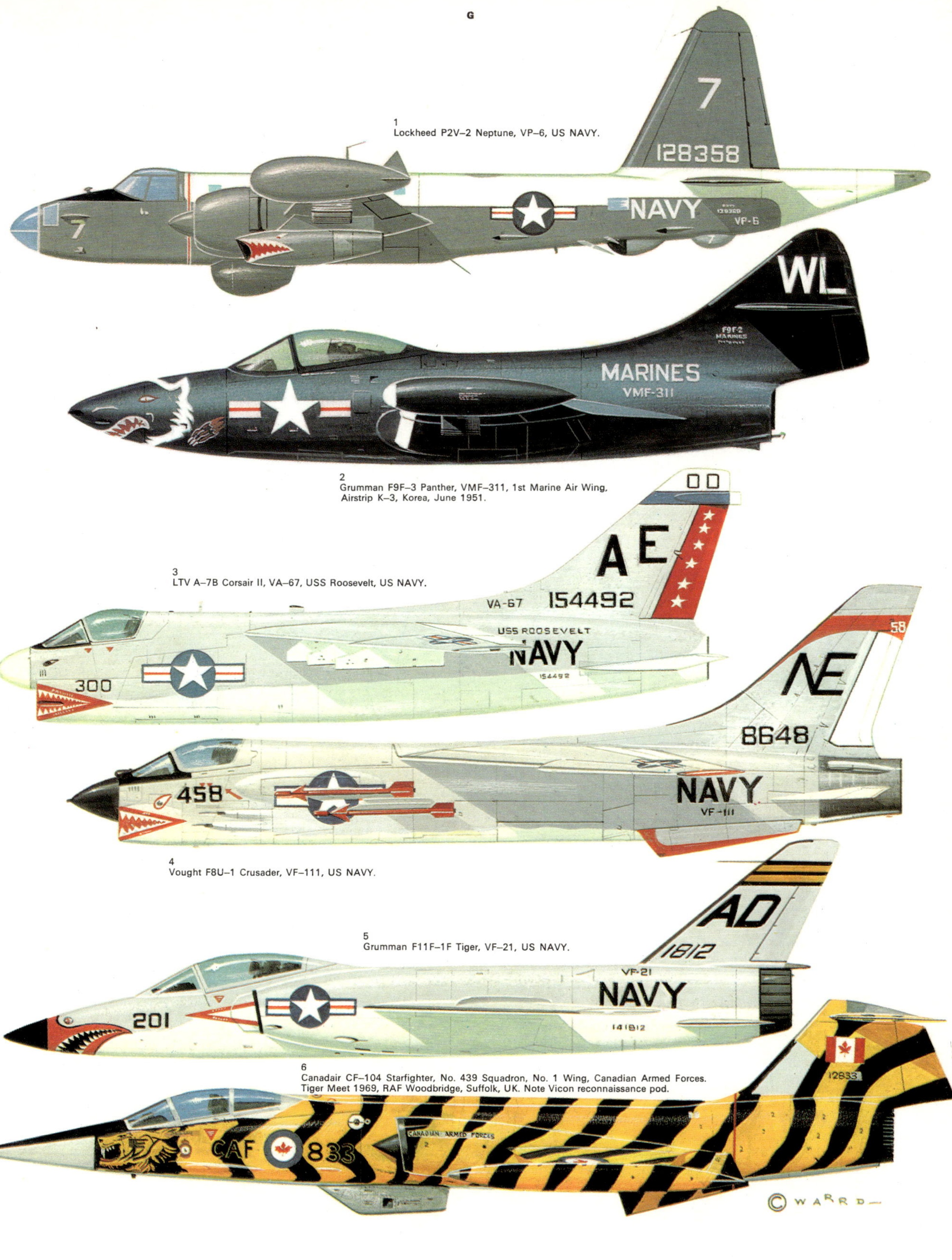

1
Lockheed P2V–2 Neptune, VP–6, US NAVY.

2
Grumman F9F–3 Panther, VMF–311, 1st Marine Air Wing,
Airstrip K–3, Korea, June 1951.

3
LTV A–7B Corsair II, VA–67, USS Roosevelt, US NAVY.

4
Vought F8U–1 Crusader, VF–111, US NAVY.

5
Grumman F11F–1F Tiger, VF–21, US NAVY.

6
Canadair CF–104 Starfighter, No. 439 Squadron, No. 1 Wing, Canadian Armed Forces.
Tiger Meet 1969, RAF Woodbridge, Suffolk, UK. Note Vicon reconnaissance pod.

1
De Havilland Tiger Moth, used as a communication aircraft by an 8th Air Force Fighter Group, ETO. 'El Pisstopho Jr'.

2
De Havilland Tiger Moth, Royal Canadian Navy.

3
North American T–6G Texan, EALA 13/72, Paul Cazelle Base, Essaouira, Central Algeria, 1957. Escadrille Commander's aircraft.

4
Cessna O1–E Bird Dog, 19th Tactical Air Support Squadron, Bien Hoa AB., South Vietnam. December 1965.

5
North American T–28D, Republic of Vietnam Air Force.

1
Consolidated B—24J Liberator, formating aircraft, 458th Bomb Group, 8th Air Force, ETO.

2
Consolidated B—24J Liberator, 458th Bomb Group, 8th Air Force, ETO.

3
Consolidated B—24J Liberator, 458th Bomb Group, 8th Air Force, ETO.

4
Consolidated B—24J Liberator, 90th Bomb Group, 5th Air Force, SWPA.

5
Consolidated B—24L Liberator, unit unknown, India, 1945.

6
Consolidated Liberator GR.VI, No. 321 Squadron, Koninklijke Marine, Netherlands East Indies. Serial unknown.

Above: De Havilland Vampire FB.5 of No. 112 'Shark' Squadron, 2nd Tactical Air Force, RAF. Photograph illustrates the C.O's aircraft WA331 complete with Sharkmouth and Helwan Cat on the fin and rudder, see colour illustration. RAF Fassburg, Germany, March 1951.

Above: Neat formation by Canadair Sabre F.4's of No. 112 'Shark' Squadron. This photo and the one below were taken shortly after the Shark-mouth was first applied to the squadron aircraft, even so X is without the marking.

Left: Close-up detail of the Sabre Sharkmouth.

Below: K XB920 is believed to have been the first Sabre to carry the marking and is shown here as the first aircraft of a squadron line-up at RAF, Bruggen, Germany, during either January or February 1955.

Above: Fine flying shot of a pair of Sabre F.4's of No. 112 'Shark' Squadron, RAF. See colour illustration of G. (RAF)

Above: Canadair Sabre F.4 and Hawker Hunter F.4 formating over RAF Bruggen. Serial number of K is XB920. The mouth on this particular Sabre is certainly black with thin red lips. (RAF)

Below: Hunter F.4 of No. 112 'Shark' Squadron being refuelled at Bruggen. (R. A. Brown)

Above: Two views of XF319 '?' flown by Sqn/Ldr H. R. Wilson, Commanding Officer of No. 112 'Shark' Squadron. Note red '?' on nose-wheel door.

Above: Hunter T in front of the squadron hanger at RAF Bruggen, Germany. It was the usual practice to paint the a/c letter on the nose-wheel door.

Right: Good detail shot of the Sharkmouth on the nose of a Hunter F.4. Although a very accurate template was used when the Sharkmouth was painted on the Hunters any small variation in the actual position of the mouth could produce problems as gun-packs were exchangeable between aircraft and sometimes the pack from one aircraft would not fit the design on another. (R. A. Brown)

Two good close-ups of the Hunter Sharkmouth, the above view shows armed gunpacks being fitted, note gun blast round the canon ports; the lower view shows the 'Sabrinas' to good advantage. (R. A. Brown)

Above: Line-up of Hunter F.4's outside the hanger at Bruggen.

Above: Hunter in for overhaul.

Left: Nose detail with cockpit and engine covers in position.

Below: Sharkmouth detail showing gunpack from a different aircraft, note variations. (Photos R. A. Brown)

Above: Republic RF–84F Thunderflash of No. 729 Tactical Reconnaissance Squadron, Royal Danish Air Force. Standard scheme of green and grey upper surfaces, pale blue/grey under surfaces, black anti-glare panel. Black mouth with white teeth. Karup, 29th August 1959. A colour illustration of another RF–84F of No. 729 Squadron will be found in AIRCAM No. 14 together with plan view details. (L. B. Hansen)

Left: Close-up detail of the Sharkmouth long-range tanks on KA–D. (Jacob Stoppel)

Below: Fiat G.91R/3 of LEKG 41, Luftwaffe. The Sharkmouth marking was temporarily applied to the aircraft of LEKG 41 during the period of the NATO Bulls Eye Competition during the summer of 1969. See colour illustration. (Gerhard Joos)

Below: Fiat G.91R/3 of the Portuguese Air Force. Colour scheme same as Luftwaffe aircraft above, mouth red, teeth white with black lips. (Juan Arraez Cerda via Mario Roberto vaz Carneiro)

Above: North American F—86K Sabre of No. 337 Squadron, Royal Norwegian Air Force. See colour illustration. (S. P. Peltz)

Below: Another Sabre of No. 337 Squadron, colour details exactly the same as for ZK—O except for black radome on nose, note different mouth details. (G. Cattaneo)

Below: F—86K Sabre also of No. 337 Squadron, Royal Norwegian Air Force, note change in squadron code. Colours as for O above, note variation in Sharkmouth. (S. P. Peltz)

Below: A pair of Dassault M.D.450 Ouragan fighters of the Israeli Defence Force/Air Force. Upper aircraft in natural metal with black/red mouth and eye, lower aircraft as colour illustration but without Suez stripes.

Above & below: Certainly not a Sharkmouth but at least one of the largest tiger heads ever painted on an aircraft. Good clear port and starboard views of the CF–104 Starfighter of No. 439 Squadron, Canadian Armed Forces, specially painted for the Tiger Meet at Woodbridge, August 1969. (Photos S. P. Peltz)

Below: Lockheed P–80A Shooting Star on display at Sampson Air Force Base, New York, 1953–4. Note non standard fin markings. (D. W. Menard)

Below: North American F–86F Sabre of the 51st Fighter Interceptor Wing, Tsuiki Air Base, Japan, 1954. (G. J. Letzter)

Above & below: Port and starboard views of a Lockheed F—94B, see colour illustration. (Upper Peter M. Bowers, lower H. J. Nowarra)

Below: North American F—86D Sabre of the 408th Fighter Interceptor Wing, 520th Fighter Interceptor Squadron, Air Defence Command, Klamath MA, Oregon. See colour illustration (USAF)

Above: North American F–100D Super Sabre of the 3rd Tactical Fighter Wing, 308th Tactical Fighter Squadron, Bien Hoa Air Base, South Vietnam, December 1965. Note 110 bombs on nose in black, 'Pakokee Tiger' on blue disc below windscreen and squadron insignia below cockpit.

Above: Nose detail showing mouth, eye, mission score and personal insignia. The aircraft is safely dispersed in one of the anti-blast pens on Bien Hoa AB. (Photos G. J. Letzter)

Below: North American F–100C Super Sabre of the 127th Tactical Fighter Squadron, Kansas Air National Guard, McConnell Air Force Base, Kansas, 1969. In standard USAF three-tone colour scheme, note 'SUE' in white on long-range tank. (Jerry Geer)

Above: Line-up of Republic F–105D Thunderchiefs of the 23rd Tactical Fighter Wing, a far cry from the Tomahawks of the Flying Tigers in the CBI. The dark green bands visible on the second aircraft are exercise markings. McConnell Air Force Base, Kansas, 1964.

Below: McDonnell F–4E Phantom of the 4531st Tactical Fighter Wing, personal aircraft of the C.O., home station Homstead AFB, Florida. Photos taken at Andrews AFB January 10th 1969. (Joseph G. Handleman)

Above: Colour details of this F–4E which arrived too late for inclusion on the colour pages are: standard USAF three-tone camouflage, black/red mouth, white teeth, black lips. Red eye on white both outlined in black. 'City of Homstead' in white on engine intake. Top of fin red with white trim repeated on side of outer long-range tank. Note inboard tank also carries a Sharkmouth. White ZD on fin with below AF67 in black followed by 320 in white, serial being 67–320. (Joseph G. Handleman)

Above: Close-up of Sharkmouth detail on F–4E.

Below: Lockheed P2V–2 Neptune of VP–6, US Navy, see colour illustration. (Duane A. Kasulka)

Above: Nice shot of a Grumman F11F–1F Tiger of VF–21, US Navy. Serial 141803, the last four repeated at base of fin, otherwise identical to the colour illustration of 201. (US Navy)

Below: Vought YF–8A Crusader at the Naval Aircraft Development Center, Johnsville, during 1965. (R. W. Harrison)

Below: Vought F8U–1 Crusader of VF–32, US Navy. See title page for colour details (G. J. Letzter)

Below: LTV A–7B Corsair II, VA–67, USS Roosevelt, see colour illustration. (Ken Buchanan)

Above: Excellent formation shot of Grumman F11F-1F Tigers of VF-21. The lead aircraft, which is the subject for the colour illustration, is trailing smoke from each wing tip. Note marking details on the upper surface of the wings. (Grumman Aerospace Corporation)

Below: A trio of Bell AH-1G HueyCobras at about maximum altitude (13,000 ft) over the Mekong Delta, South Vietnam. These ships are operated in the Vietnam Delta area by the 1st Squad, 7th Cavalry, US Army. Custer might have found the addition of a few HueyCobras useful in staving off his final come-uppance in the Black Hills of South Dakota! (Bell Helicopter Company)

Below: Close-up of the Sharkmouth on the turret and nose of a Bell AH-1G gunship of the 7th Cavalry. (Note Cavalry 'Crossed Swords' insignia in yellow under nose) See side-view illustration for colour details (Bell Helicopter Company)

Above: A Sharkmouthed Bell AH–1G from one of the aviation battalions attached to the 25th Infantry Division in South Vietnam. Note the white 'eunoch' insignia aft of cockpit. (US Army)

Below: Bell AH–1G HueyCobra of the 7th Cavalry Division, South Vietnam. Green drab camouflage overall, red mouth, white teeth, red and white eye. Small black anti-glare panel ahead of cockpit, lettering black. Tips of main blades yellow, tail blades red/white/red, both hubs natural metal. Cavalry 'Crossed Swords' insignia under nose.

Below: North American OV–10A Bronco of VMO–1 at MCAS New River, North Carolina. Medium green upper surfaces, pale grey under surfaces, ER and 205 in white, all other lettering black, Marines on fuselage, serial 155484 on fin with OV–10A above. Red 'Hornet' face area with white mouth outlined black, red teeth, black/white eye, black eyebrow, white spinner with red stripes.

Below left: North American OV–10A Bronco of VMO–1 showing off its 'Hornets Mouth' which was only carried by the Bronco for a very brief period towards the end of 1969. (North American)

Below right: Sharkmouthed Marine LCI; Marines are shown making a dress rehearsal landing at Taupota Bay, New Georgia Island in the Southwest Pacific. (USMC)

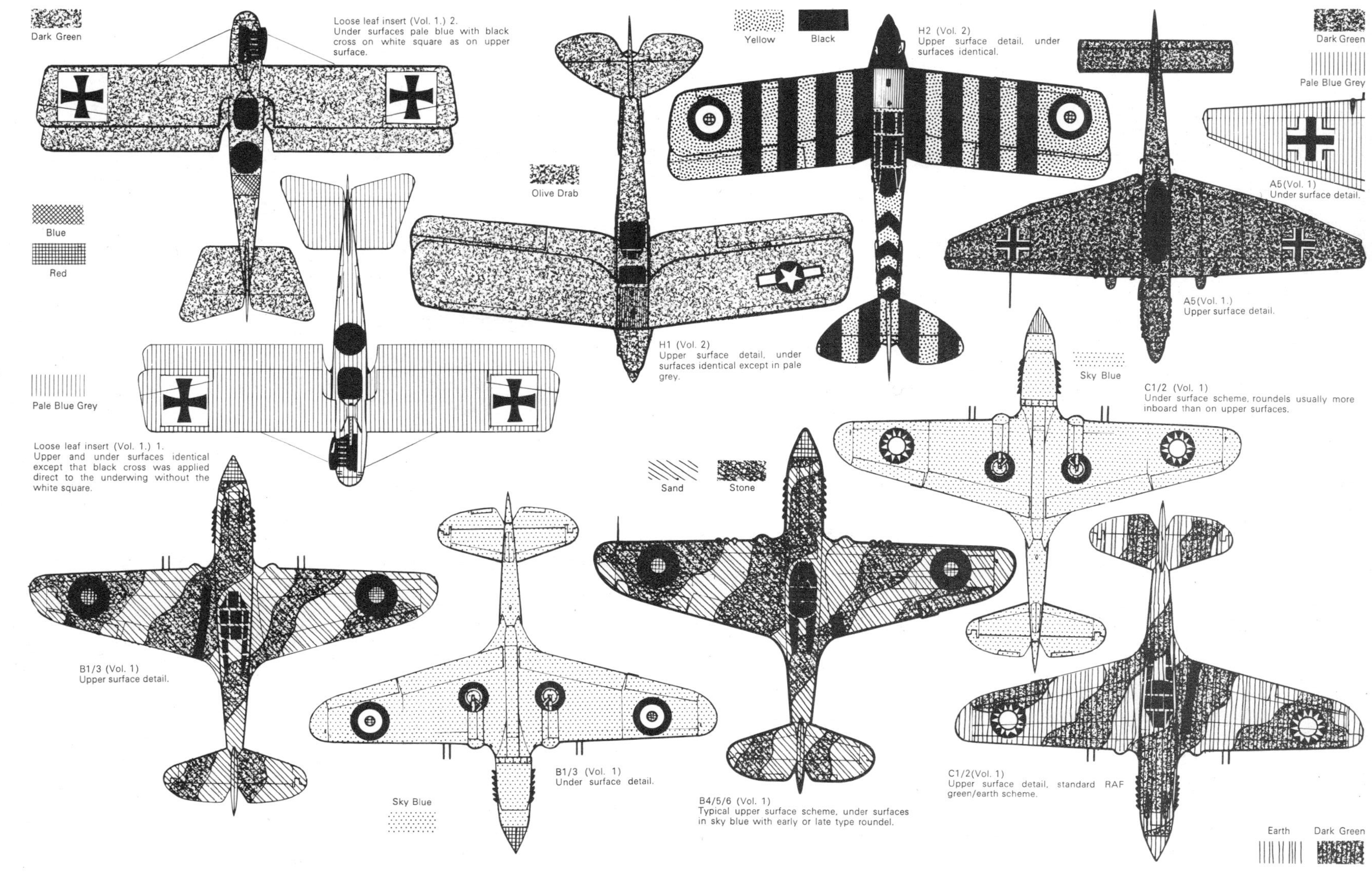

Dark Green
Loose leaf insert (Vol. 1.) 2. Under surfaces pale blue with black cross on white square as on upper surface.
Yellow
Black
H2 (Vol. 2) Upper surface detail, under surfaces identical.
Dark Green
Pale Blue Grey
A5 (Vol. 1) Under surface detail.
Blue
Red
Olive Drab
Pale Blue Grey
H1 (Vol. 2) Upper surface detail, under surfaces identical except in pale grey.
A5 (Vol. 1.) Upper surface detail.
Loose leaf insert (Vol. 1.) 1. Upper and under surfaces identical except that black cross was applied direct to the underwing without the white square.
Sky Blue
C1/2 (Vol. 1) Under surface scheme, roundels usually more inboard than on upper surfaces.
Sand
Stone
B1/3 (Vol. 1) Upper surface detail.
B1/3 (Vol. 1) Under surface detail.
B4/5/6 (Vol. 1) Typical upper surface scheme, under surfaces in sky blue with early or late type roundel.
C1/2 (Vol. 1) Upper surface detail, standard RAF green/earth scheme.
Sky Blue
Earth
Dark Green

Olive Drab
Grey
F5 (Vol. 1)
Under surface with standard D-Day stripes.
Black
Dark Olive Drab
H5 (Vol. 1)
Upper surface detail, under surfaces identical except in pale blue.
H4 (Vol. 1)
Upper surface detail, note red is shown black.
Olive Green
Red
C4 (Vol. 1)
Standard USAAF upper and under surfaces of OD and pale grey. All other Warhawks conform to the standard RAF Desert scheme for which see B1/3 and B4/5/6 (Vol. 1), insignia in standard positions.
F4/5 (Vol. 1)
Standard upper surface scheme, standard under surface pale grey.
Pale Grey
Yellow
E2 (Vol. 1)
Upper surface scheme.
H4 (Vol. 1)
Under surface detail, note white band does not extend over flap.
Silver Dope
E2 (Vol. 1)
Under surface scheme.
H6 (Vol. 1)
Upper surface detail, under surfaces identical except in pale blue.
H3 (Vol. 1)
Upper surface scheme, under surfaces in pale blue, red star without white outline.
Olive Green
H3 (Vol. 2)
Upper surface and under surface details identical.
F1 (Vol. 1)
RAF green/earth upper surfaces with pale blue under surfaces: F2 in standard USAAF OD and grey scheme with US ARMY under wings.
Green
Earth
Grey
Green
G1 (Vol. 1)
Note: With and without white leading edge to the wings: Upper surface detail, under surfaces identical except in pale grey
Earth
Green
Yellow